A Paines Plough and Belgr

Hungry

by Chris Bush

Supported using public funding by
ARTS COUNCIL ENGLAND

Hungry

by Chris Bush

Cast

LORI	Eleanor Sutton
BEX	Leah St Luce

Production Team

Director	Katie Posner
Designer	Lydia Denno
Lighting Designer	Richard Howell
Sound Designer	Kieran Lucas
Movement Director	Kloe Dean
Assistant Director	Kaleya Baxe
Dramaturg	Sarah Dickenson
Casting Director	Jacob Sparrow
Costume Supervisor	Rhiannon Hawthorn
Movement Support	Esme Benjamin
Lighting Programmer	Sam Ohlsson
Company Stage Manager	Aime Neeme
Technical Stage Manager	Benjamin Smith, Philip Thackray
Stage Management Support	Ruth Porter
With thanks to	V&A Productions
	Abbie Morgan

CHRIS BUSH (Writer)

Chris is an award-winning playwright, lyricist, theatre-maker and an Associate Director at Sheffield Theatres. Previously for Paines Plough: TRUE NORTH (part of Come To Where I Am). Other past work includes STANDING AT THE SKY'S EDGE (Sheffield Theatres – Best Theatre: South Bank Sky Arts Awards, Best Musical: UK Theatre Awards), NINE LESSONS AND CAROLS: STORIES FOR A LONG WINTER (Almeida Theatre), FAUSTUS: THAT DAMNED WOMAN (Headlong/Lyric Hammersmith/ Birmingham Rep), THE LAST NOËL (Attic Theatre/UK tour), THE ASSASSINATION OF KATIE HOPKINS (Theatr Clwyd – Best Musical: UK Theatre Awards), PERICLES (National Theatre: Olivier), THE CHANGING ROOM (NT Connections), THE BAND PLAYS ON, STEEL, WHAT WE WISHED FOR, A DREAM, THE SHEFFIELD MYSTERIES (all Sheffield Theatres), SCENES FROM THE END OF THE WORLD (Yard/Central School), A DECLARATION FROM THE PEOPLE (National Theatre: Dorfman), LARKSONG (New Vic, Stoke-on-Trent), SPEAKING FREELY, POKING THE BEAR (both Theatre503), THE BUREAU OF LOST THINGS (Theatre503/Rose Bruford) and ODD (Perfect Pitch/Royal & Derngate Northampton). Awards/prizes include a South Bank Sky Arts Award, two UK Theatre Awards, the Perfect Pitch Award, a Brit Writers' Award and the Theatre Royal Haymarket Writers' Award.

ELEANOR SUTTON (Lori)

Eleanor's theatre credits include: THE CRUCIBLE and A LITTLE NIGHT MUSIC (Chester Storyhouse); AMADEUS (National Theatre); FUTURE CONDITIONAL (The Old Vic); THE MASTER BUILDER (The Old Vic); THE WIZARD OF OZ (Leeds Playhouse); WINDOWS (Finborough Theatre) and AS YOU LIKE IT (UK tour).

LEAH ST LUCE (Bex)

Training: Urdang Academy & The Brit School. Stage Credits: Cover Alice/Tom Cat in DICK WHITTINGTON (National Theatre), Little Eva/Shirelle/Ensemble in BEAUTIFUL (UK Tour), Kathy / Ensemble / Cover Judy in 9 TO 5 The Musical (UK & Ireland Tour), Lisa in MAMMA MIA! (Novello Theatre), Ensemble in CINDERELLA (Chris Hallam, Greenwich Theatre), Corrine in COME BACK AND GONE (Claire Grove, BBC Radio 4), Zonia in JOE TURNER'S COME AND GONE (David Lan, The Young Vic), OLIVER! (Cameron Mackintosh), Patty in HANDLE AND SPOUT (Cartoonito Karaoke), Young Nala in DISNEY'S THE LION KING (Lyceum Theatre).

KATIE POSNER (Director)

Katie joined Paines Plough as Joint Artistic Director with Charlotte Bennett in August 2019. She is currently directing the Paines Plough Roundabout 2021 season, which includes HUNGRY by Chris Bush, REALLY BIG AND REALLY LOUD by Phoebe Eclair-Powell and BLACK LOVE by Chinonyerem Odimba, which she is co-directing with Chinonyerem Odimba. Katie is an experienced and award-winning director. She has worked across a wide variety of productions both overseas and on national tours, including multiple productions with York Theatre Royal and Pilot Theatre with whom she was Associate Director from 2009 until 2017. Her work encompasses both intimate pieces of new writing and larger-scale community pieces. In 2019 Katie received a UK Theatre Award nomination as Best Director with her production of MY MOTHER SAID I NEVER SHOULD at Theatre By The Lake. Recent productions include: MY MOTHER SAID I NEVER SHOULD (Theatre By The Lake), MOLD RIOTS (Theatr Clwyd) and THE SEVEN AGES OF PATIENCE (Kiln Theatre). Recent credits include: SWALLOWS & AMAZONS (Storyhouse), BABE (Mercury Theatre), PLAYING UP (NYT), FINDING NANA (New Perspectives), MADE IN INDIA (Tamasha, Belgrade, Pilot), EVERYTHING IS POSSIBLE: THE YORK SUFFRAGETTES (York Theatre Royal), THE SEASON TICKET (Northern Stage), A VIEW FROM ISLINGTON NORTH (Out Of Joint), IN FOG AND FALLING SNOW (National

Railway Museum), RUNNING ON THE CRACKS (Tron Theatre), END OF DESIRE (York Theatre Royal), YORK MYSTERY PLAYS (Museum Gardens York), BLACKBIRD, GHOST TOWN, CLOCKING IN, A RESTLESS PLACE (Pilot Theatre).

LYDIA DENNO (Designer)

Lydia is a visual artist. She studied Theatre Design at Nottingham Trent and graduated in 2007. She began her career as assistant designer on the award-winning Railway Children (National Railway Museum and King's Cross Theatre), and has gone on to develop an interdisciplinary practice which encompasses theatre, installation, illustration and even walking. She has worked for theatres such as York Theatre Royal, Nottingham Playhouse, The Lowry, Soho Theatre and Wembley Arena, as well as heritage sites around the UK and galleries internationally. Lydia's design work has been awarded an Eastern Eye Award and recently 'gained laurels' having been selected for the Tribeca Film Festival. She is excited by the stories that spaces and objects can tell, as well as the people that inhabit and use them. With Iraqi-British heritage, she is interested in cross-cultural storytelling and in particular stories that transcend physical and metaphysical borders. She is drawn towards under-represented stories and characters, interested in fleeting moments and gestures as performance, and enticed by what narratives lie in the detail.

RICHARD HOWELL (Lighting Designer)

Richard trained at Guildhall School of Music and Drama. Credits include: TARTUFFE, CORIOLANUS (RSC); THE WRITER (Almeida); ARISTOCRATS, PRIVACY (Donmar); ALL MY SONS, JEKYLL AND HYDE (Old Vic, London); PINTER 5 & 6, GLENGARRY GLEN ROSS, BAD JEWS, KILLER JOE (West End); I SEE YOU (Royal Court, Jerwood Theatre Upstairs); HOMECOMING, EAST IS EAST (Trafalgar Studios for Jamie Lloyd Company); CAT ON A HOT TIN ROOF, BREAKING THE CODE, A DOLL'S HOUSE, LITTLE SHOP OF HORRORS (Manchester Royal Exchange); LABYRINTH (Hampstead Theatre); THE COUNTRY WIFE (Chichester, Minerva); THE WILD PARTY (The Other Palace); FAUSTUS, THE GLASS MENAGERIE (Headlong, UK Tour); A MIDSUMMER NIGHT'S DREAM, THE WIZARD OF OZ, PLAYING FOR TIME (Sheffield Crucible); THE GRINNING MAN, THE CRUCIBLE, THE LIFE AND TIMES OF FANNY HILL (Bristol Old Vic); THE MADNESS OF GEORGE III (Nottingham Playhouse); PROJECT POLUNIN (Sadlers Wells); CABARET (Gothenburg Opera); BREAKING THE WAVES, FLIGHT (Scottish Opera); IL TRITTICO, MADAME BUTTERFLY, LA FANCIULLA (Opera Holland Park); MADAME BUTTERFLY (Danish National Opera).

KIERAN LUCAS (Sound Designer)

Kieran is an award-nominated sound designer & theatre-maker. He is a founding member of Barrel Organ & associate artist at Coney. Credits include: THE FUTURE PROJECT (Streatham Space Project), FOUND SOUND (Coventry Creates/Coventry City of Culture), NOAH & THE PEACOCK (Nottingham Playhouse), ME FOR THE WORLD (Young Vic), THE RAGE OF NARCISSUS (Pleasance Islington), ANTIGONE (New Diorama), GASTRONOMIC (Shoreditch Town Hall/Norwich Theatre Royal), CONSPIRACY (Underbelly/New Diorama), POPS (HighTide Festival) COMPANION: MOON (Natural History Museum), HOW WE SAVE THE WORLD (Natural History Museum), THE EX-BOYFRIEND YARD SALE (CPT/Progress Festival), TBCTV (Somerset House), SQUARE GO (Paines Plough Roundabout/59E59), A GIRL IN SCHOOL UNIFORM (Walks Into A Bar) (New Diorama), MY NAME IS RACHEL CORRIE (Young Vic), BIG GUNS (The Yard), UNDER THE SKIN (St Paul's Cathedral).

KLOE DEAN (Movement Director)

Kloe is a Choreographer, Movement Director and Performing Artist from London, UK, specialising in hip-hop, funk and streetdance styles. Kloe is a Work Place artist at The Place, Kings Cross, Creative Director of all-female hip-hop dance company, Myself UK Dance, and has presented a range of dance theatre both nationally and internationally including Breakin Convention in London, Ladies Of Hip Hop in New York and The Sub Urban Danse Festival Copenhagen. Kloé has worked with a range of music artists including Little Simz, Cleo Sol and Rita Ora, as well as brands such as Jimmy Choo, Nike, Marks & Spencer's and George at ASDA.

KALEYA BAXE (Assistant Director)

Kaleya Baxe is a writer, director and facilitator whose work is driven by her passion for representation, inclusion and a collaborative process. As well as working on outreach and youth projects with the Young Vic, Kiln, Arcola Theatre and several drama schools, her work often shines a light on important subjects (PATRICIA GETS READY (FOR A DATE WITH THE MAN THAT USED TO HIT HER) and has toured schools, youth settings and pupil referral units (WRITTEN, Little Fish Theatre). As an assistant she has worked with acclaimed writers such as Chinonyerem Odimba (Artistic Director, Tiata Fahodzi) and Mike Bartlett (Doctor Foster, Life). Kaleya trained at the Royal Central School of Speech and Drama on the Drama, Applied Theatre and Education course. Her work as a director includes; 786 by Ric Renton (Paines Plough R&D, LAMDA), PATRICIA GETS READY (FOR A DATE WITH THE MAN THAT USED TO HIT HER) by Martha Watson Allpress (Pleasance, VAULT Festival Show of the Week Award Winner) and WRITTEN by Alex Cooke (Little Fish Theatre, Schools and Youth Settings Tour).

AIME NEEME (Company Stage Manager)

Aime is a LAMDA trained freelance theatre director and stage manager. Past credits include; PARAKEET (Boundless), HARD FEELINGS, THE HOTEL PLAYS, A LIE OF THE MIND (Defibrillator Theatre), DENNIS OF PENGE (Ovalhouse).

BENJAMIN SMITH (Technical Stage Manager)

Benjamin graduated from the Stage Management and Technical Theatre course at the Royal Welsh College of Music and Drama in 2018. Since leaving he has had a varied work career, Sound Designing, Re-Lighting, as well as both Technical and Company Stage Management. Previous work includes: JANE EYRE (Blackeyed Theatre), ANIMAL FARM (Pegasus Theatre), ANNA KARENINA (Pegasus Theatre), UNFORTUNATE (Fat Rascal Theatre), VULVARINE (Fat Rascal Theatre), WORD GET'S AROUND (RCT Theatre), MEMORY OF WATER (ALRA North), 2023 (Illumine Theatre Company).

PHILIP THACKRAY (Technical Stage Manager)

Philip Thackray is one of this technical stage managers for this year's Roundabout tour, having worked previously on the 2019 Roundabout tour and a large background in fringe theatre and outdoor events. Phil currently works as freelance theatre and live event technician having worked often with Theatr Clywd on a number of their productions and with T-bats for their outdoor events. Credits-Technical Crew ROUNDABOUT TOUR - 2019. Senior Build Crew and Senior Event Supervisor GUNG HO tour 2018, 2019. Stage Technician 2018 HANSEL & GRETEL: FAIRYTALE DETECTIVES -Theatr Clywd.

 **Paines Plough**

Paines Plough are a touring theatre company dedicated to new writing; we find, develop and empower writers across the country and share their explosive new stories with audiences all over the UK and beyond.

'The lifeblood of the UK's theatre ecosystem.' *Guardian*

Since 1974 Paines Plough has worked with over 300 outstanding British playwrights including James Graham, Sarah Kane, Dennis Kelly, Mike Bartlett, Sam Steiner, Elinor Cook, Vinay Patel, Zia Ahmed and Kae Tempest.

Our plays are nationally identified and locally heard. We tour to over 40 places a year and are committed to bringing work to communities who might not otherwise have the opportunity to experience much new writing or theatre. We reach over 30,000 people annually from Cornwall to the Orkney Islands, in village halls and in our own pop-up theatre Roundabout; a state of the art, in the round auditorium which travels the length and breadth of the country.

'That noble company Paines Plough, de facto national theatre of new writing.' *Daily Telegraph*

Furthering our reach beyond theatre walls our audio app COME TO WHERE I'M FROM hosts 180 original mini plays about home and our digital projects connect with audiences via WhatsApp, phone, email and even by post.

Wherever you are, you can experience a Paines Plough Production.

'I think some theatre just saved my life.' @kate_clement on Twitter

Paines Plough Limited is a company limited by guarantee and a registered charity.
Registered Company no: 1165130
Registered Charity no: 267523

Paines Plough, 2nd Floor, 10 Leake Street, London SE1 7NN
+ 44 (0) 20 7240 4533

office@painesplough.com
www.painesplough.com

Follow @PainesPlough on Twitter
Follow @painesplough on Instagram
Like Paines Plough at facebook.com/PainesPloughHQ
Donate to Paines Plough at justgiving.com/PainesPlough

ROUNDABOUT

'A beautifully designed masterpiece in engineering' *The Stage*

ROUNDABOUT is Paines Plough's beautiful portable in-the-round theatre. It's a completely self-contained 168-seat auditorium that flat packs into a single lorry and pops up anywhere from theatres to school halls, sports centres, warehouses, car parks and fields.

We built ROUNDABOUT to tour to places that don't have theatres. ROUNDABOUT travels the length and breadth of the UK bringing the nation's best playwrights and a thrilling theatrical experience to audiences everywhere.

Over the last six years ROUNDABOUT has hosted over 2,000 hours of entertainment for more than 100,000 people in places ranging from a churchyard in Salford to Margate seafront.

ROUNDABOUT was designed by Lucy Osborne and Emma Chapman at Studio Three Sixty in collaboration with Charcoalblue and Howard Eaton.

WINNER of Theatre Building of the Year at The Stage Awards 2014

'ROUNDABOUT venue wins most beautiful interior venue by far @edfringe.'

@ChaoticKirsty on Twitter

'ROUNDABOUT is a beautiful, magical space. Hidden tech make it Turkish-bath-tranquil but with circus-tent-cheek. Aces.'

@evenicol on Twitter

ROUNDABOUT was made possible thanks to the belief and generous support of the following Trusts and individuals and all who named a seat in Roundabout. We thank them all.

TRUSTS AND FOUNDATIONS
Andrew Lloyd Webber Foundation
Paul Hamlyn Foundation
Garfield Weston Foundation
J Paul Getty Jnr Charitable Trust
John Ellerman Foundation

CORPORATE
Universal Consolidated Group
Howard Eaton Lighting Ltd
Charcoalblue
Avolites Ltd
Factory Settings
Total Solutions

Roundabout is supported by the Theatres Trust in 2021.

Theatres Trust

Pop your name on a seat and help us pop-up around the UK:
www.justgiving.com/fundraising/roundaboutauditorium

Paines Plough

Joint Artistic Directors and CEOs	Charlotte Bennett & Katie Posner
Executive Producer	Holly Gladwell
Technical Director	Colin Everitt
Producer	Matt Maltby
Associate Producer	Christabel Holmes
Marketing and Audience Development Manager	Jo Langdon
Marketing Manager	Cherise Cross
New Work Associate	Phillippe Cato
Community Engagement Manager	Jasmyn Fisher-Ryner
Digital Producer	Nick Virk
The Big Room Playwright Fellow 2020	Vickie Donoghue
The Big Room Playwright Fellow 2021	Mufaro Makubika
The Big Room Playwright Bursary Recipient	Ric Renton
Trainee Director	Kaleya Baxe
Trainee Producer	Ellen Larson
Marketing Trainee	Molly Goetzee

Board of Directors

Ankur Bahl, Corey Campbell, Kim Grant (Chair), Asma Hussain, Tarek Iskander, Olivier Pierre-Noël, Cindy Polemis, Carolyn Saunders, Laura Wade

Supported using public funding by
ARTS COUNCIL ENGLAND

Belgrade
Theatre
Coventry

Together, with the diverse communities across Coventry and the region, we aim to enrich and fundamentally change people's lives for the better through theatre.

In our landmark building, across the region, the UK and online, we will use theatre to entertain, inspire, share the city's stories, uncover hidden histories and unleash the creativity in our communities.

The Belgrade is the largest professional theatre in Coventry and so we act as both the city and region's commercial and producing theatre. We are also highly respected for our ground-breaking community and education initiatives. Hamish Glen is the current Artistic Director and Chief Executive.

The Belgrade is a registered charity and receives revenue funding from Coventry City Council and Arts Council England as well as project funding from these and other government sources.

The Belgrade played a key role in securing Coventry as UK City of Culture 2021 and in 2019 we appointed Corey Campbell, Balisha Karra and Justine Themen as Co-Artistic Directors, with a remit to programme and direct the Theatre's produced work for UK City of Culture 2021.

Senior Management Team:

Hamish Glen
CHIEF EXECUTIVE & ARTISTIC DIRECTOR

Joanna Reid
EXECUTIVE DIRECTOR

Corey Campbell
2021 CO-ARTISTIC DIRECTOR

Balisha Karra
2021 CO-ARTISTIC DIRECTOR

Justine Themen
2021 CO-ARTISTIC DIRECTOR

Sâmir Bhamra
2021 SENIOR PRODUCER

Vera Ding
GENERAL MANAGER

Adrian Sweeney
DIRECTOR OF PRODUCTION

Richard Hope-Jones
GENERAL MANAGER – BPS

Nicola Young
DIRECTOR OF COMMUNICATIONS

Ray Clenshaw
COMMUNICATIONS MANAGER

Helen Hotchkiss
HEAD OF DEVELOPMENT

Paul Newsome
FINANCIAL CONTROLLER

HUNGRY

Chris Bush

For Roni,
my food explorer

Foreword
Chris Bush

Food is my love language. At one point I thought that if I didn't
write for a living, I might want to cook instead. Admittedly that
was a stupid idea – I don't have the temperament for a
professional kitchen – but few things make me happier than
navigating a hot stove (so long as things are going well). Over
the years I've constructed extravagant gingerbread houses and
prepared multi-course tasting menus, I even made my sister's
wedding cake – a ten-tier topographic map of the Bakewell
valley, with the flavours of a Bakewell tart. The construction of
said cake did almost give me a nervous breakdown, but it was
absolutely worth it. If I'm not able to bake for day one of
rehearsals, something has gone seriously wrong. I still have a
sticky and battered copy of Nigella Lawson's *How to Be a
Domestic Goddess* which was gifted to me by the cast of my
first university production. I have a fridge full of homemade
pickles (sitting alongside the obligatory sourdough starter), a
financially irresponsible collection of Le Creuset and an
overflowing box of postcards where I transcribe noteworthy
recipes plucked from the internet or my imagination.

One of the few things I enjoy more than cooking is eating. If
some people eat to live, while others live to eat, I definitely fall
into the latter category. When deciding where to travel abroad,
food is always top of my list. My tastes are broad, and not
always refined. A friend once described me as eating like a dog
does – not stopping when I'm full, but continuing until no more
food remains, regardless of the quantity. He wasn't entirely
wrong. Like so many people, I've often struggled with my
weight. I've indulged and denied myself in ways that weren't
always healthy. I still find it challenging to reconcile my natural
greed and the complicated relationship I have with my body. I
want to try everything once, and then go back for seconds. I
will never be the one to turn down dessert. My willpower is

often non-existent. I don't want to be the kind of person who counts calories, and yet on occasion I do. I weigh out sad little recommended portions of unrefined carbohydrates and restrict myself to buying meat or fish once a fortnight. I have taken one of my greatest pleasures and placed a series of restrictions upon it, against all my better instincts, because I grudgingly accept that certain pleasures come at a cost. On paper I applaud anyone who espouses 'eat what you want, when you want', but maybe I just don't trust myself enough not to take this to excess. I'm not sure whether this makes me miserable or sensible, or maybe a little bit of both. It's complicated.

Food is incredibly emotive. Taste and smell are powerful and nostalgic senses, possessing the ability to transport us through space and time in a mouthful. There might be a proper explanation for this that involves brain chemistry, but we don't need one. There's a reason why so many great dramas play out around the dinner table, and leading supermarkets run ad campaigns about 'food love stories'. What tastes better than a meal prepared by someone who adores you? When we cook for our loved ones, we're offering up a piece of ourselves on a plate. A bit of our culture, perhaps, or our imagination, our aspirations, our taste. The more we make an effort, the more we make ourselves vulnerable. We want to dazzle, to impress, we heap pressure on fancy dinners to save faltering relationships, or beg forgiveness with elaborate apology breakfasts. We say 'I know this is your favourite' or 'I thought you might like this.' We say 'I care' or 'I remembered.' We offer up our last Rolo. That's love.

Hungry is a love story of sorts – a love story told through food – but it isn't necessarily a healthy one. For all the romanticised notions I have of showing affection through culinary enterprise, I also wanted to explore the deeply toxic nature of our relationship with what we consume. Food isn't just emotive because we use it to show we care; it's also used to assign value and pass judgement. In a line cut from an earlier draft: 'You are what you eat – show me your fridge and I'll show you what you're worth.' It's a truism that the cheapest and easiest food to prepare often has the least nutritional value. A 'poor' diet is rarely just the result of poor choices, but is undeniably affected by class and financial precarity, along with a whole host of other factors. As we're increasingly encouraged to be responsible and 'eat better' – to spend more on organic, small-batch, cruelty-free produce which can never be scaled up to feed the general population – we inch ever closer to a two-tier system where the one per cent can continue to eat what they want with a clear conscience, and the proletariat make do with their nutritionally enriched gruel. (If this sounds like hyperbole, a brief look at the world of 'food replacement systems' might convince you otherwise. Not only is the product already here, but it's being marketed as aspirational.) The recent school-dinners scandal clearly illustrates a world of difference between what those in charge deem good enough for the most vulnerable, and what they're prepared to eat themselves.

I don't have ready-made solutions to any of this, but anyone interested in reading more about the subject would do well to start with Ruby Tandoh and Jack Monroe. I also found Felicity Lawrence's *Not On the Label* and Jay Rayner's *A Greedy Man in a Hungry World* to be extremely useful and accessible introductions to our dysfunctional food system. The story of Bex and Lori started out back in 2013, when I started writing a very different version of this play while on attachment at Sheffield Theatres. I never quite cracked it then, but something about the themes and those characters stuck with me, and when discussing ideas with Katie and Charlotte for the Roundabout I jumped at the chance to return to them. I'm grateful to Daniel Evans for his help on that earlier version, Sarah Dickenson for her expert dramaturgical guidance, Katie Posner for her exquisite direction, Leah and Eleanor for their truly beautiful, delicate performances, and the entire Paines Plough team for their superhuman efforts in bringing this piece to the stage. Thanks also to my fabulous agents Matt and Alex, and all at Nick Hern Books. I'd also like to take this moment to pay tribute to the resilience of the whole theatre industry, who have had eighteen months of hell. We're not out of the woods yet by any means, but if you're holding this in your hands a small miracle has occurred, and for that I'm very grateful.

Oh, and Nigella, thank you for everything.

Bon appétit.

July 2021

Characters

BEX, *twenty-two, black*

LORI, *late twenties/early thirties, white*

Note

There are two distinct modes in this play – NOW and THEN. It's useful for us to always know when we're in the present and when we're in the past.

In the present, Bex and Lori are setting up for a gathering. This plays out almost in real time.

The scenes in the past span a couple of years.

This play went to press before the end of rehearsals and so may differ slightly from the play as performed.

1. THEN

LORI. Service!

BEX *appears*.

This way round, yeah? Spoons at two o'clock.

BEX. Sorry?

LORI. Towards the diner, not you.

BEX (*glancing at her watch*). It's nine-thirty.

LORI. What?

BEX. The time, it's –

LORI. The plate.

BEX. What about it?

LORI. Seriously? (*Sighs.*) Okay, so a clockface – picture a clockface –

BEX. Why?

LORI. That's the plate – the plate is the clock. Spoon at two o'clock – like this – when it goes in front of them. Now go.

BEX. Show me once more.

LORI. Plate. Spoon. Clock. Spoon is the hand.

BEX. Big hand or little hand?

LORI. Big hand! Big hand at –

BEX. Thing is I'm more digital.

LORI. It isn't –

BEX *can't keep this up any longer. She cracks up.*

BEX. Your face.

LORI. Right.

BEX. I'm on it. I'm Bex, by the way.

LORI. I'm busy.

BEX. Okay.

LORI. And these are melting.

BEX. Got it.

LORI. So you can dick around on your own time, yeah? Not while we're in service.

BEX. Yes, chef.

LORI. You get that? This is a time-sensitive operation. I'm not… Can you just take them please?

BEX. Sorry. I wasn't –

LORI. Now, please.

BEX. Yep.

   BEX *starts to go*.

LORI. I'm Lori. It's Lori.

BEX (*smiles*). Yes, chef.

   Into –

2. NOW

BEX. What've you got there?

LORI. Sandwiches.

BEX. Why?

LORI. I said I'd bring sandwiches.

BEX. And I said I had it covered.

LORI. I don't mind.

BEX. I do. What is that?

LORI. Chicken.

BEX. Is it though?

LORI. Yes! It's a turmeric chicken with Scotch bonnet aioli and a kohlrabi slaw.

BEX. Why is it black?

LORI. It's an activated-charcoal flatbread.

BEX. No food should be black.

LORI. It's dramatic.

BEX. No one's going to eat that.

LORI. You'll like it. It's practically Nando's. (*Beat*.) Try one. It's the same dressing we use on the ribs.

BEX. I'm not hungry, thank you.

LORI. It's nice.

BEX. I know it'll be nice. It's not about *nice*, it's about Mum.

LORI. I know. It's only chicken.

BEX. Is it though?

LORI. And some pulled jackfruit for the vegetarians.

BEX. We don't know any vegetarians.

LORI. How is that possible?

BEX *shrugs*.

It's here now, anyway. It was no bother.

BEX. I didn't ask you to.

LORI. Didn't have to. (*Beat*.) Y'know this could be a good, um, proof of concept for us as well. See what they make of it, because it's this sort of thing –

BEX. Use my family as guinea pigs?

LORI. Not like… But a customer base –

BEX. So that's why you're here?

LORI. No! I'm sorry. No. I'm here for you.

BEX. Okay.

LORI. It is. It's going to be okay.

Beat.

BEX. Give them here then – I'll get them in the fridge.

BEX *takes the tray. Into –*

3. THEN

LORI. Clean plates?

BEX. Clean plates, big grins.

LORI. Good.

BEX. What was the green gunk again?

LORI. Excuse me?

BEX. Y'know – the dribble round the edge.

LORI. That is a basil fluid gel.

BEX. On a pudding?

LORI. Any complaints?

BEX. No, just someone asking.

LORI. They liked it then?

BEX. Yeah – oh yeah – too much if anything. Had this one old dude telling me how chocolate was a… a what-do-you-call-it – an aphrodisiac.

LORI. Jesus.

BEX. Then he tried to sit me on his knee and feed me a spoonful of his mousse.

LORI. Marquise.

BEX. Hmm?

LORI. Not a mousse – it was a chocolate marquise.

BEX. I think you're missing the point of the story.

LORI. Did you tell people it was a mousse?

BEX. Did I tell you he had a visible erection?

LORI. Anyway – thank you for tonight.

BEX. No bother.

LORI. There's not much left to do. You could start wiping down the sides for me?

BEX. Sure.

LORI. And take a drink if you want one – open bottles over there.

BEX. We allowed?

LORI. No, but if we don't it has to go down the sink, which is criminal, so...

BEX. Right.

LORI. Go on – the white tastes like piss but the red's decent.

BEX. Nah, you're alright. Is there a boiling water tap in here though?

LORI. What're you after? I think the tea and coffee got packed away, but –

BEX. No, just... I've got a Pot Noodle in my bag.

LORI. Excuse me?

BEX. Didn't get a chance to eat before we started, so –

LORI. Are you serious?

BEX. I'll keep my fork at two o'clock, if that helps.

LORI. Absolutely not. Not on my watch.

BEX. Oh. (*Beat*.) Right, um. That's fine. I'll have it when I get home. Sorry.

LORI. You will not – you'll chuck it in the bin where it belongs. Now – any allergies – intolerances? Real ones, not made up.

BEX. What's happening right now?

LORI. You don't bring a Pot Noodle into a professional chef's kitchen – it's an insult.

BEX. Sorry.

LORI. I should hope so. You clear those counters – I'm making you a snack.

BEX. Nah –

LORI. Five minutes.

BEX. Seriously?

LORI. It's my civic duty.

BEX. You must be knackered. Everything's packed away –

LORI. Just do as you're told and stop answering back, alright?

BEX (*with a smile*). Yes, chef.

LORI. And pour me another red. Five minutes and I'm going to blow your mind.

Into –

4. NOW

LORI. When do they get here?

BEX. Soon. Should be soon. Dad said he'd only take them for one, but...

LORI. They in The York?

BEX. Yeah.

LORI. You didn't want to?

BEX. Hmm?

LORI. Join them? We could go and –

BEX. Nah.

LORI. You could, I mean. Go have a drink – leave me to sort everything here.

BEX. Everything's sorted, so.

LORI. I just mean you can leave me by myself – put me to work – you don't have to worry about me.

BEX. I'm not worried about you.

LORI. Okay.

BEX. I'm not worrying about you.

LORI. I just meant if you wanted to go –

BEX. Then I'd be there, wouldn't I? I wouldn't be waiting for your permission.

LORI. Sorry.

   BEX *doesn't entirely accept the apology.*

   Just tell me what I can do. Anything you need, just…
   (*Pause.*) What am I today?

BEX. How do you mean?

LORI. I wasn't sure whether… Am I a friend, or co-worker, or – ?

BEX. Oh.

LORI. I don't mind if –

BEX. No – no, girlfriend. Girlfriend is… That's fine.

LORI. Yeah?

BEX. Yeah. They're not… That's not a problem.

LORI. Okay. Good. (*Beat*.) Good that... not good that I'm still your girlfriend, although that is good, but good that it isn't –

BEX. Can we not – ?

LORI. I just didn't know whether all your family – if extended family – whether that might be –

BEX. They're not dickheads.

LORI. I just wasn't sure.

BEX. If they were dickheads?

LORI. What the deal was, that's all.

BEX. Got it.

LORI. So if it was easier to just be platonic-work-friend-business-partner-tea-lady then...

BEX. Then what?

LORI. That'd be fine.

BEX. That'd be weird.

LORI. Whatever you need. Today is about you –

BEX. Today's about Mum.

LORI. Yeah.

BEX. But she's dead, so. (*Pause*.) You don't have to be here. I didn't ask you to be here. So if you're not up for an afternoon of small talk with my possibly homophobic relatives you can just unwrap your fruit platters and piss off.

LORI (*softly*). Whatever you need.

BEX. They're fine though, actually – for the record. For a bunch of dickheads.

LORI. I don't think your family are dickheads.

BEX. Yeah, well you've not met them all yet.

LORI. What can I do?

BEX. Go. Stay. Suit yourself. I've got to get on.

Into –

5. THEN

BEX (*brightly*). Hey!

LORI. Hey! You again!

BEX. Me again. You miss me?

LORI. Uh –

BEX. It's Bex.

LORI. I know. I know, I hadn't –

BEX. It's okay. Lori, yeah?

LORI. Yeah.

BEX. Queen of the Midnight Feast. Blew my mind. Just like you promised.

LORI. Right.

BEX. You don't even remember!

LORI. No –

BEX. Bet you do it for all the girls.

LORI (*blushing, trying to move past this*). Great. So. Great to have you back on the team. Do you know what we're doing tonight?

BEX. Is it serving dinner?

LORI. So it's going to be really easy on you guys. We've got a series of sequential sharing plates for structured grazing. It's all plant-based and low-carbon.

BEX. Uh-huh.

LORI. Everything comes from within a fifty-mile radius of the kitchen – a lot of it's grown right here. All our suppliers are listed. We've got hand-outs for anyone who asks. Did you have any questions?

BEX. Yes. What exactly is the heritage of the heritage tomatoes?

LORI. Is that a real question?

BEX. Are they related to the Queen, or – ?

LORI. Any serious questions?

BEX. Did Prince Charles grow them?

LORI. They come from Essex and they're organic and they're very good.

BEX. What do they taste of?

LORI. Tomatoes.

BEX. Got it.

LORI. You'll be serving some ingredients you're unfamiliar with. If you're asked something you don't know don't guess, check in with the kitchen, yeah?

BEX. Oh, one other thing – pickled turnip, sprout tops and cobnuts?

LORI. What about them?

BEX. Bet you a fiver no one touches it.

LORI *thinks for a second*.

LORI. You're on.

BEX. So what're you going to make me tonight then?

LORI *(ignoring this)*. First plates go out at six, on the dot. The trout's chilled and the kitchen's hot, so I need you to be on it.

BEX. Yes, chef.

LORI. Anything else?

BEX. No one likes cold fish either.

LORI. Tuck your shirt in. Are those the shoes you're wearing?

BEX. Looks like it.

LORI. Okay. Try to keep up. It's going to be a long night.

Into –

6. NOW

LORI *is fixing* BEX*'s collar or picking a bit of fluff off her sleeve.*

BEX. What're you doing?

LORI. Making you respectable.

BEX. Good luck.

LORI (*clocking her shirt*). Have you ironed this?

BEX. Doesn't need ironing.

LORI. It absolutely does.

BEX. It's fine.

LORI. Will there be one here?

BEX. What?

LORI. An iron?

BEX. No one cares.

LORI. No, *you* don't care.

BEX. No one's going to care today.

LORI. They will! Someone will tut or frown or give you a funny look and then… I'll do it – I don't mind doing it. Pass it here.

BEX. You trying to get my clothes off already?

LORI (*deadpan*). You saw right through me. Strip off.

BEX. Make me.

LORI. Bex –

BEX. Look at me. All crumpled. I'm a disgrace.

LORI. I wasn't –

BEX. Come teach me a lesson.

> BEX *pulls* LORI *towards her, her hands on her shirt. Into* –

7. THEN

BEX *and* LORI *have just had sex. They kiss.*

LORI. Jesus.

BEX. You okay?

LORI. Yeah.

BEX. You sure?

LORI. Yeah, I'm… Wow. I might just need a… (*Beat – a new thought.*) Oh, before I forget –

> LORI *rummages around in her pockets until she finds a five-pound note – she tosses it towards* BEX.

BEX. Uh, what the fuck?

LORI. What? (*Realising.*) Oh, shit, no – cobnuts –

BEX. What?

LORI. Fucking pickled-turnip bullshit.

BEX. Oh!

> *They are both now near hysterical.*

LORI. From the… Nobody touched it.

BEX. Right.

LORI. I wasn't –

BEX. No.

LORI. Sorry.

BEX. I did wonder. For a second.

LORI. I'm really sorry.

BEX. Thought 'wow, I've misread this.'

LORI. I just – I saw the jar of cobnuts up on the shelf.

BEX. Right.

LORI. It reminded me.

BEX. And honestly, if I was charging I reckon a fiver seems quite low.

LORI. Yeah. Yeah, absolutely. I mean I wouldn't know, but –

BEX. I mean, I'll still take it.

They giggle again.

LORI. They really hated that dish.

BEX. Told you so.

LORI. It tastes good! (*Off her look.*) It does – I swear! Did you try it?

BEX *doesn't answer.*

Right – you're going to taste it now.

BEX. You're alright.

LORI. Just a mouthful.

BEX. I've already eaten.

LORI *gives her a look.*

I do shifts for Ollie at The Lime Tree sometimes. He does
charred sprouts with bacon and chimichurri. They banged.

LORI. Right.

BEX. I mean if you pick the sprouts out and just eat the bacon.

LORI. Ollie's a hack.

BEX. Just saying. Problem is your pickles. You do pickles and
greens you need something richer than a cobnut to balance it.
Something creamy or fatty, something emulsified. (*Beat.*)
What? Don't worry, I'll give you some pointers next time
and we won't end up scraping so much of it into the bins.
Cos it's not very eco, is it – all that wastage?

LORI. Shall we have another drink?

BEX. I'm okay.

LORI. Are you sure? I think I might. Do you mind? I just…
I don't make a habit of this. To be clear.

BEX. Right.

LORI. I've never… This isn't the kind of thing I do.

BEX. That's a shame.

LORI. Was it okay?

BEX. More than okay.

LORI. No, I mean okay like… You didn't feel pressured?
I wasn't abusing my power?

BEX. What power?

LORI. You were working for me tonight.

BEX. Yes, chef.

LORI. It wasn't inappropriate to – ?

BEX. Was fingering me in the walk-in fridge inappropriate?

LORI. I just –

BEX. For a workplace environment?

LORI. I wouldn't want to… I'd hate it if you –

BEX. I was off the clock. (*Beat*.) I don't make a habit of it either. So you know.

LORI. Have another drink with me. Just one, just… Come on. This is not a… a normal shift, and I would like to… Something nice. Let's open some two-hundred-pound, some five-hundred-pound bottle of… Write it off as a breakage. Get some waiter fired. Martin, maybe. Twat. I would like a paddling pool of claret. A swimming pool – an Olympic swimming pool full of… Do you know about the wine lake? There used to be a wine lake somewhere. And a butter mountain. In Europe. All the excess – all the extra… Because of the… the… the EU – the restrictions on… So they'd end up with all this surplus, just piled up somewhere. I'd like to go live in the butter mountain. Go skiing down the butter mountain. Smear myself in it. Not in a… You're thinking in a sexy way but that's not how I mean it. That's your mind. I mean it very wholesomely actually. I want the freshest bread and the creamiest butter and the reddest wine. I want a pain de campagne the size of a double bed, rip the crust off while it's warm and soft and just snuggle up inside it. Butter pillow. Butter bedsheets. Bed and butter. Breakfast in bread. Is that…? I'm not drunk, I just haven't eaten today. Bread and butter and wine – that's all you need. Not all this faff – 'dining concepts' – trends and tweezers – and no pickled turnips, I promise. No cold fish. Just bread and butter and wine – and you. What bread do you buy? This is important. Do you buy good bread? You have to buy the best you can. Not from a supermarket – never – not even the Finest, the Taste the Difference – no – *real* bread. No plastic shit. You are never to eat shit bread again, do you understand me? I'm serious. I forbid it. I'll never buy you flowers because flowers are pointless – you just sit them there and watch them die – but I will bake for you, any hour of the day or night. I'd watch you eat. I'd eat you up. Look at you. You get it, don't you? You're *real*. You know what matters. Simple things. Bread and butter and wine and you. Sorry. I'm being weird. I thought I was being romantic but I'm just being drunk and gay. Do you want something to eat?

8. NOW

BEX *has just (half-heartedly) come on to* LORI. *It's awkward.*

BEX. Right. Forget it.

LORI. Sorry.

BEX. Doesn't matter.

LORI. I wasn't... Just because of how we left things, whether –

BEX. Yeah.

LORI. Or if... if... People could be back any minute, you said – your dad, so –

BEX. Not exactly the best time for a quickie.

LORI. No.

BEX. Stupid. I'm stupid.

LORI. You're not.

BEX. I am.

LORI. Come here –

BEX *moves away.*

BEX. I just thought... y'know, you said 'anything' – anything I needed, so...

LORI. Yeah. Okay, yeah.

BEX. And maybe it would bash some of the sad out of my head for five minutes, but... You're right. Bad idea.

LORI. I'm sorry.

BEX. It's fine.

LORI. We have... How much time do you think we have?

BEX. Moment's gone.

LORI. We could make out for a minute. Or just cuddle? Might be nice to –

BEX. It's alright.

LORI. It's just that you said space – to give you space – not to… And that's been really hard.

BEX. Sorry.

LORI. I'm not saying be sorry, I just… I wanted to come round sooner. I did. (*Beat.*) I was glad when you invited me today.

BEX. Yeah, well. Didn't ask you to cater it, but…

LORI. It's good to see you. Come here. (*Beat.*) Please. If that's okay.

BEX *moves towards* LORI. BEX *allows herself to be held.*

You've lost weight.

BEX. Have I?

LORI. I think so, yeah.

BEX. Do I need to change?

LORI. No, you're fine. You're great.

BEX. It's one of those shirts you don't have to iron, actually.

LORI. Right.

BEX. That's what the label says.

LORI. You're lovely. You look lovely.

Into –

9. THEN

BEX. You're wearing a skirt.

LORI. I am, yeah.

BEX. Should I have worn a skirt? Is this a skirt place?

LORI. You look great.

BEX. Is this a dickhead place?

LORI. It's nice. You're going to like it.

BEX. If you'd told me where we were going –

LORI. It's a surprise.

BEX. You just said seaside. So I thought layers.

LORI. Felix is a mate. You can wear whatever you like. (*Beat.*)
Now, we've got the wine flight with dinner, but did you want
a cocktail to start?

BEX. You didn't have to do all this.

LORI. I wanted to. Champagne, obviously the classic choice
with oysters, but a trailblazer such as myself might do a Fino
sherry –

BEX. I don't do oysters.

LORI. First time for everything. Ooh – or Black Velvets!
Guinness and champagne cocktails – have you ever…? (*To
an unseen waiter.*) Hi! Incredible. And can we get two Black
Velvets and two glasses of the Valdespino? Brilliant. (*To
BEX.*) I figure you try both, and I'll just drink whatever's left
over. (*Beat.*) Go on.

BEX. Do I have to?

LORI. They're not a punishment, they're a rite of passage.
They're a proper aphrodisiac – you know that?

BEX. Says who?

LORI. Everyone. Very sexy. Very erotic.

BEX. How are these sexy?

LORI. You know – because they look like a…

BEX. A what?

LORI. You know!

BEX. A fanny?!

LORI. Ugh!

BEX *cackles*.

BEX. Really?

LORI. Yes!

BEX. Do they though? Do you think they do?

LORI. I don't know. Maybe.

BEX. What kind of fucked-up fannies have you been looking at?

LORI. It's a thing!

BEX. Is that what my fanny looks like to you?

LORI. It's just a thing – a known thing – that they're said to…
    Oysters, clams, any kind of… bivalve.

BEX. Bivalve?

LORI. Try one.

BEX. Is that why you like them? Why you're so proficient?

LORI. Stop it.

BEX. Dab hand with them – know how to open them up, give
    them a good slurp –

LORI. Alright –

BEX. A pro with a clam, hasn't got a clue what to do with a
    carrot.

    LORI *looks away.*

    Do I taste like an oyster? (*Beat.*) Because that's a thing, isn't
    it? About girls tasting fishy. Which is – don't get me wrong –
    actually just bullshit peddled by incels with a fear of
    cunnilingus – but – fish isn't meant to be that fishy either, is
    it? You go into a fishmongers and it reeks of fish, you know
    something's wrong. It's supposed to smell of the sea. Do I
    taste of the sea?

LORI. Try one and see for yourself.

    BEX *considers it.*

BEX. Ugh, no, I can't.

LORI. How will you know whether you like it until you try it?

BEX. You know that's the argument my first boyfriend used to talk me into anal.

LORI. Fine. Fuck it – fine – do whatever you want.

BEX. Are you mad at me?

LORI. I'm just trying to… There is a world beyond chicken nuggets, you know?

BEX. Nothing wrong with a chicken nugget.

LORI. No, actually there is.

BEX. Agree to disagree.

LORI. I'm trying to do something nice. Something special. I let you rip the piss when we're working but actually I've put a lot of thought and time and money, as it happens, into tonight, so I could really do without… It isn't cute. It's actually really boring when you're like this. It makes you seem small.

BEX. Okay.

LORI. Not like… I didn't… Are you drinking that?

BEX *shrugs a 'go ahead'.*

Let me try again. Have I told you about Normandy? Normandy. I was fourteen. First ever time abroad. We were flat broke back then, but my parents had been saving up for years. A proper holiday. Massive deal. We're staying in some shitty tumbledown BnB where we all got fleas – genuinely – and it's rained the whole week, but then on the last night we go down to this little place on the harbour and the air is warm and the stars are out and Dad says I can order anything I like. I want oysters. I don't know what they are exactly, but I want them, and we've got this cartoon of a snooty French waiter who gives us this look like 'fuck off, all of you – she doesn't want them – he can't afford them', which just makes both of us more determined, so out they come, and I don't know what I was expecting, but I try one and it's just... They taste of everything I didn't even know I wanted. Magic. Unforgettable. I want you to have that. I wanted us to sit by the window so you can see the sea and the boats coming in and it's there – it's *right there*.

BEX. They're that good then?

LORI. I want you to experience things you never otherwise would, because I think... You turn your nose up at all this because you think it's not for you, but it is – it can be for you! You deserve it! You're special! But waiting tables isn't special. Chicken nuggets aren't special. The life you have right now isn't special and it should be. (*Beat.*) Forget it.

BEX. Right then.

LORI. I'm sorry.

BEX. Okay, you slippery bitch. Let's see what all the fuss is about.

LORI. You don't have to.

BEX. Do you just sort of knock it back, or – ?

LORI. Leave it.

BEX. I want to.

LORI. No, you don't.

BEX. No, I don't, but I'm going to. Just... (*Still dithering with the oyster.*) Just for the record though – this isn't normal. Oysters aren't normal. Having a spiritual experience with seafood aged fourteen isn't a normal thing to do.

LORI. I don't think you're normal either.

BEX. And it's a myth about chicken nuggets – McDonald's did those ads. There's nothing weird in them, just chicken.

LORI. Doesn't matter. Genuinely. Just leave it.

    BEX *does*.

BEX. You should have them. You love them – you have them.

LORI. I'm not going to sit and eat a plate of oysters all by myself – I'll feel like a Roman emperor or something.

BEX. Okay.

Pause.

LORI. I've really fucked this, haven't I?

BEX. No! No, it's going to be great. (*Beat.*) It's not all raw, is it?

LORI. No.

BEX. Good. (*Beat.*) Thank you for... I'm sorry. And anything you put in front of me from now on, I'll eat it, I promise. I'll do better. I'm excited.

LORI. You hate it here.

BEX. It's perfect.

LORI. No, it's perfect for me. I should've known –

BEX. I love it.

LORI. You called it a dickhead place.

BEX. I'm sorry.

LORI. Come on – let's go.

BEX. What?

LORI. I mean it. We're going.

BEX. Haven't we got like six courses left?

LORI. Doesn't matter. What time is it? (*Glances at her watch.*) Good. Still plenty of light. We're having fish and chips on the beach. We're going to The Seagull because they use proper beef dripping and we're going to wait and make them cook it from fresh. We're going to pick up two bottles of prosecco from M&S on the way.

BEX. We can do that any time.

LORI. But we're doing it now. Three bottles – one for me, one for you, one for the road. And we'll come back here later for pudding and cocktails at the bar. All the fucking puddings. Just normal, delicious puddings. And all the booze.

BEX. Won't your mate mind?

LORI. No. I'm going to get him to put a sparkler in it and everything. I'm going to make everyone sing.

BEX. I will hate that.

LORI. You've got to give me something.

BEX. You've planned a whole thing.

LORI. I'm going rogue.

BEX. You're wearing a skirt.

LORI. So you'd better remove it at the earliest opportunity.

BEX. It won't be special.

LORI. It's with you – of course it's special.

BEX. I'm sorry.

LORI. What for?

BEX. Spoiling things.

LORI. You've not spoiled anything. I love you.

BEX. What?

LORI. You heard me.

BEX. Say that again.

LORI. I love you. No biggie. And you don't have to say it back
   if –

BEX. I love you too.

LORI. Happy birthday.

   BEX *smiles. Into –*

10. NOW

BEX. What else have you brought then?

LORI. Nothing. (*Beat*.) Barely anything. A couple of salads. Some more fruit.

BEX (*without enthusiasm*). Great.

LORI. And some of those home-made peanut-butter-cup things.

BEX. The ones that tasted of sand?

LORI. Just thought it'd be good to have a bit of variety. (*Beat*.) Are you eating? Properly eating, not...? I could do some meal prep, bring some things round.

BEX. We're fine.

LORI. I'd like to.

BEX. We've got every auntie for fifty miles bringing us casseroles, we're alright.

LORI. Okay, good. That's good. (*Beat*.) Just for balance though. Something with veg, pulses, the proper stuff. Maybe just for the freezer – for you and your dad, so –

BEX. Freezer's full.

LORI. What if we had a sort through? Because it's probably all her stuff, isn't it? You don't have to eat like that any more. We could –

BEX. Stop it.

LORI. I just mean you can have a bit more control now – over what you –

BEX. Right.

LORI. Might be good. Might be liberating.

BEX. Uh-huh.

LORI. In your own time. Whenever you're ready. Just to –

BEX. I won't end up like her.

LORI. I know.

BEX. Isn't that what you're afraid of?

LORI. I never –

BEX. I'll reach forty and just… The look on your face the first time you met. You tried to hide it, but I saw. We didn't have sex for a fortnight afterwards, did you know that?

LORI. She was an incredible woman.

BEX. Who ate herself to death?

LORI. I… I know she struggled with…

BEX. I'm not chucking anything out. It's all good – won't waste it. There was some pretty green malt loaf in the back of her dresser, but otherwise…

LORI. Okay.

BEX. I'm still finding her little stashes – thought I knew them all. Cheesy Wotsits in the airing cupboard, Jammy Dodgers under the bathroom sink. Pulled out a box marked 'Christmas baubles' and it was just full of Matchmakers.

LORI. Classic.

BEX. I wish she was catering this. She'd have known exactly what to put out – how to get everyone smiling. How many meals – thousands – tens of thousands – served at this table and no one ever left it hungry. Can you always say that?

LORI. Tell me what you need.

BEX. I need my mum.

LORI. Why don't you sit down for a minute? Just sit still for a minute and… What have you eaten today?

BEX. I'm fine.

LORI. Let me fix you a little plate, just to keep you going. Something simple.

BEX. I'm really not hungry.

Into –

11. THEN

LORI *has just got in*. BEX *is in high spirits*.

LORI. What is all this?

BEX. You alright?

LORI. What're you doing?

BEX. Wouldn't you like to know? There's beer in the fridge.
Those fancy Dutch ones you like.

LORI. What for?

BEX. If you're not pissed already?

LORI. I just had the one closing down.

BEX. Well, I hope you didn't eat.

LORI. No.

BEX. Good.

> BEX *pulls* LORI *in for a kiss*.

> I'm cooking.

LORI. You don't cook.

BEX. I'm expanding my horizons.

LORI. I could've brought something back.

BEX. I know. Fish stew – Normandy-style. Got Anton to give
me some instruction on the sly. Look – nothing frozen – all
fresh. He did the filleting for me, cos I didn't fancy the trip to
A&E, but one step at a time.

LORI. Okay…

BEX. Grab a beer. Go on. No shortcuts, no packets, no artificial
whatever. All responsible and sustainable. And check this out –
pain de campagne – the good stuff, from that beardy place. And
I'm going to toast crumbs of it in garlic butter – real French
butter – and then you sprinkle them on top. Had to do a test run
to get it right and they're fucking incredible. Oh – and a green-
bean salad too, to stop it getting too lardy – very balanced.

LORI. Right. (*Beat.*) Sorry, am I missing something?

BEX. How do you mean?

LORI. I haven't… It's not an anniversary, or – ?

BEX. No.

LORI. Then what?

BEX. And then – the pièce de résistance, slightly less on-theme – Rice Krispie brownies. Sounds trashy, but it's actually a Nigella thing, and Nigella is the only white woman I truly trust, so.

LORI. Wow. Stone cold.

BEX. I would let her do things to me.

LORI. Is everything alright?

BEX. Do you want to taste? Tell me if it needs any…? No – don't actually. I'm feeling good. I want to get it right by myself.

LORI. Y'know what, this looks… incredible. Like actually incredible.

BEX. Try not to sound so surprised.

LORI. What happened?

BEX. Had a day off.

LORI. Yeah, but –

BEX. It's only dinner.

LORI. No, it isn't.

BEX. I dunno. You're always telling me I have these hidden depths and I'm not saying you're right or anything but…

LORI *smiles*.

Shut up! You've not tasted it yet. Lower your expectations. And don't look at anything too closely, it's a state, just… I know you have this catalogue in your head of every meal that's changed your life, and so I thought, well, if I'm serious about us maybe it's time I made the list.

LORI. Thank you.

BEX. But you can't watch me. Sit down. Put your feet up. I've got it all covered.

LORI. Yes, chef.

Into –

12. NOW

BEX. You do know you're like two hours early?

LORI. Sorry?

BEX. And obviously everyone else will be late.

LORI. I wanted to help set up.

BEX. I didn't ask for that.

LORI. You don't have to.

BEX. I told you it was covered. I was super clear. I said this is the deal – come pay respects or whatever – and you said 'can I bring anything?' and I said no, and you said it's no bother and I said no, and then you said sandwiches, and I said no – I've got it covered.

LORI. I just thought –

BEX. What?

LORI. Maybe you'd –

BEX. Have fucked it all and need rescuing?

LORI. Maybe you wouldn't want to be alone. (*Beat.*) Maybe you'd have successfully banished everyone else, but actually when it came down to it you could use some company from someone who doesn't mind it when you scream at them.

Maybe I'm the last person you'd want to see but I'd still be
better than no one.

Pause.

BEX. Doesn't mean I want your fruit platter.

LORI. Your mum used to love my fruit platters. (*Off her look.*)
She did! Never touched them herself but she said they made
her look good – put one out every time she had a house visit.
She told me.

BEX *isn't amused.*

Oh, I know she hated me. (*Beat.*) That's okay. It's not like
I've got a pathological need for approval or anything.

BEX (*grudgingly*). She didn't hate you.

LORI. She used to call me 'skinny flat white'.

BEX *laughs.*

I've had worse. (*Beat.*) I wish she could've seen it – the
restaurant. She'd have been so proud. Not that she wasn't
proud of you already, but –

BEX. She wouldn't be seen dead.

LORI. She'd have loved it. (*Beat.*) I've got some other bits and
pieces in the van too. Business stuff. Nothing important,
just… If you could sign the lease agreement though, it means
I can start hiring contractors.

BEX. Right.

LORI. Just a signature, that's all. Because everything's in both
our names. But I brought some of the fun stuff too –
branding mock-ups, sample menus – just in case. I emailed
you, but –

BEX. I saw. Haven't looked yet.

LORI. Okay.

BEX. Sorry.

LORI. That's okay. Just wanted to keep you in the loop. Looks even better in the flesh, so… I think Kerry's really come through.

BEX. Great.

Beat.

LORI. Anyway, you tell me – you let me know what level of involvement you're ready for with anything – no pressure – and I'll just keep cracking on.

BEX. Yeah.

LORI. If you don't let me know what you need from me I'm just going to keep guessing, which is fine, but evidently I'm not getting much right so far, so… (*Pause.*) I can't imagine what you're going through. Losing a parent is… I can't imagine. But I can listen, and I can look after you, if you'll let me, and…

BEX. I'm fine.

LORI. You're not.

BEX. Of course I'm fucking not. So what're you going to do – make me a salad?

LORI. No.

BEX. None of this helps.

LORI. If you… There's science in… If your body isn't getting what it needs it can't heal.

BEX. I know you put a lot of faith in kale, but it can't resurrect the dead, so.

LORI. I know.

BEX. Today isn't about healing. Today was never about healthy choices. Today is about eating our feelings and getting wasted and maybe even having a bit of a laugh if we can manage it, and if you're not on board with that, you really don't have to stay.

LORI. Okay.

BEX. I mean it. Might turn into a bit of a session later, so.

LORI. I'm fine.

BEX. Yeah?

LORI. I promise.

BEX. No one asked you to turn up with a stick up your arse and a van full of tofu.

LORI. I didn't know what else to do.

BEX. Right.

LORI. I cook. I cater. It is literally my job – what else was I going to do? Why wouldn't you want my help?

BEX. Because I don't need it.

LORI. Okay.

BEX. What?

LORI. I'm not going to fight with you.

BEX. Stop being a twat then.

LORI. You've done brilliantly – getting anything out is brilliant –

BEX. But?

LORI. Okay! But now we actually have some variety, not just whatever beige shit was in your freezer.

BEX. This is how I want it.

LORI. Right, so it's a... a sentimental thing, I get it – that's not a criticism. But surely it's better to have a range – have some colour –

BEX. Your chicken's black.

LORI. I've got other stuff.

BEX. And bringing black chicken to a wake – I don't know if that's you working to a theme, or –

LORI. If you'd talked to me – if you'd told me what you wanted –

BEX. I told you it was covered.

LORI. Not just the food – if you'd talked to me about anything… (*Beat*.) Do you want me here at all?

Pause. BEX *can't answer*.

Right. (*Beat*.) So why even invite me?

Pause.

BEX. I thought you were working.

Beat.

LORI. What?

BEX. I spoke to Tony and he said you were doing some big wedding this weekend – out in Hertford, Hereford, somewhere out of town. Thought you wouldn't be able to make it.

LORI. Oh.

Pause.

BEX. Sorry.

LORI. Yeah. I was, yeah. I pulled out.

BEX. Right.

LORI. I wanted to –

BEX. You must have lost –

LORI. A few thousand. (*Pause*.) I set them up with Zainab though – she could really do with it. She'll be great.

BEX. I'm sorry you did that.

LORI. I was happy to. Really happy when –

BEX. I'm sorry.

LORI. Why? (*Beat*.) I know you're dealing with a lot, but I really do think I'm allowed to ask you why now.

BEX *looks away*.

Cos I've tried to be patient, and respectful, and not to
trample over your grief or whatever. I'm not perfect, I know
that – I'm annoying as fuck sometimes – but it really has felt
like I'm being punished for something and I don't think it's
entirely fair. (*Pause.*) I've stopped drinking. Not *stopped*,
but… cutting back, anyway. So you know.

BEX. That's good.

LORI. And we've got so much planned right now – big things –
exciting things – like proper life-changing things between
the two of us that I must've done something pretty awful to
make you hate me this much.

BEX. I don't hate you.

LORI. What is it then?

BEX. My mum died.

LORI. I know.

BEX. I don't need anything else. You can go now.

Into –

13. THEN

LORI. So…?

BEX. Your own place?

LORI. Can't stay in catering forever. I'll be fucked if I'm doing
another supper club. Shoot me in the face before I buy a food
truck.

BEX. Sure.

LORI. Now's the time to get serious about it. Jonno's a wanker
but he's got cash to burn. Plus I can borrow a bit from my
parents maybe, and so many places are going to go bust in
the next year rents will be dirt cheap.

BEX. Isn't that risky?

LORI. Not if the product's right. I know I can staff the kitchen no bother, I just need someone mega to run front of house.

BEX. Right.

LORI. Someone properly brilliant. Someone I can trust.

BEX. Yeah.

LORI. Someone I can make out with in the walk-in if it gets quiet.

Beat.

BEX. You mean...?

LORI. What do you reckon?

BEX. Me?

LORI. Who else?

BEX. But... What do I know about any of that?

LORI. You'd learn.

BEX. You must need qualifications, or –

LORI. Maybe. So get them. Plenty of night courses – college courses – all that sort of... No rush – we can take our time, and you can get a grant, or a loan, or –

BEX. No, this is actually mad.

LORI. Talk to Tony. Talk to Freja, actually, because she's a total badass, and she might mentor you. Or if she can't I bet she'll know someone who could.

BEX. I still add up on my fingers, you know that?

LORI. You'll get better! What else are you doing? I can hardly have you waiting tables in my own place, can I?

BEX. Why not?

LORI. Wouldn't that be embarrassing?

BEX. For who?

LORI. Just think about it – our own place. Not mine, *ours*. Somewhere round here. Local. Unpretentious. Comfortable. Somewhere you could take your mum.

BEX (*a little wary*). Right.

LORI. I mean it. But not, y'know, not junk – still healthy and eco-conscious and sustainable, just without making a big deal about it. Big flavours – bright, fresh, punchy – and – get this – I was thinking we do Soul Food.

BEX. Really?

LORI. With our own twist. Because what is Soul Food, actually, or anything that comes out of that sort of diaspora? It's community, right? It's traditions, not trends. It's this honest sort of elbows-on-the-table, lick-your-fingers, sit yourself down and get yourself fed.

BEX. Right.

LORI. And people love it, because it's got comfort and history, but actually the exciting thing about a… a jambalaya, or a jollof, or a jerk whatever – is the flavour, right? It's only flavour –

BEX. Okay. None of those things are Soul Food though.

LORI. Don't be pedantic. It's British. Contemporary British. Which is anything. It's roasted plantain with chip-shop spice. It's Dublin Bay prawns with gumbo butter. It's… You remember that place we went with Emma for curry goat?

BEX. I think so.

LORI. So I've been working on this thing – it's a bit cheffy, sure, but you swap out the goat for hogget – British-reared – slow roast in a firepit with a spice rub then smoked over Earl Grey tea. So it's a bit Caribbean, a bit Texas barbecue, and then Earl fucking Grey – the most English thing! Magic.

BEX. Got it.

LORI. You see?

BEX. So it's just a bit of something from anywhere we've stuck a flag.

LORI. No – you can fuck off with all of that. It's *flavour*, and I understand flavour – flavour is my life. It's not *colonial* to... to expand your horizons. This is what I keep telling you. Or else you end up like my granddad, demanding liver and onions five times a week and thinking a clove of garlic is a bridge too far. That's the danger – that's the racist attitude. Racists don't eat chicken tikka masala –

BEX. I'm pretty sure they do.

LORI. Okay, they definitely do, but... Food should unite us. It's essential and universal, and it's all the same – fundamentally all the same. Protein, vegetable, carbohydrate. Salt and fat and acid and heat. No one *owns* that. We should never... 'This isn't your dish, it's mine.' 'You can't sit at our table.' No – *that* is elitist. That is the opposite of... sitting down and breaking bread and sharing something.

BEX. I'm just saying all this – this is why people don't like Jamie Oliver.

LORI. That's not why people don't like Jamie Oliver.

BEX. It's one of the reasons.

LORI. So you're not allowed pizza?

BEX. What?

LORI. You're not Italian – why are you allowed to eat pizza?

BEX. I wasn't saying that.

LORI. See – it's ridiculous. And actually, actually, white chefs *should* be learning, we *should* be looking further afield, not just idolising classical French or modern Nordic, but studying all those world cuisines banished to the deep-fat fryer and the late-night takeaway. And – and – okay, if you look at some of those cultures, those, um, people of specific ethnic backgrounds where there's a propensity towards, uh, obesity, or diabetes, or heart disease – what if that's because historically those cuisines have been neglected? What if we take them, elevate them, do something lighter, fresher, a bit different –

BEX. You want to teach my grandma how to fry chicken?

LORI. I'd probably bake it, so…

BEX *laughs at this, in spite of herself.*

BEX. You do know people will give you shit for this?

LORI. That's what I've got you for.

BEX. Can we talk about this later? Can I think about it?

LORI. Imagine we had a restaurant where your mum felt totally welcome and she could order anything on the menu without feeling bad about it. Imagine that.

BEX. Maybe.

LORI. How's she doing? You said she had another appointment?

BEX. Oh yeah. Fine. Just got her bloods checked, and a new inhaler.

LORI. And that was all – ?

BEX. Yeah, good. New doctor. Nicer than the last one.

LORI. That's good. (*Beat.*) Think about it. Just think about it. Time for a new adventure.

Back to –

14. NOW

BEX. You should find someone else for the restaurant too, obviously.

LORI. What's going on?

BEX. Shouldn't be hard. Get Emma in on it – or Zainab maybe
– your little protégé.

LORI. Don't be stupid.

BEX. Just make sure they're the right shade so no one comes
after you.

LORI. Forget about all that for now. Talk to me.

BEX. I'll see how much of a refund I can get from college. I'll
pay you back.

LORI. Have you stopped going?

BEX. I don't want you wasting any more money on me.

LORI. It's fine to take a break – just speak to them, let them
know – or I can call them, if you haven't already.

BEX. I'm not going back.

LORI. They have, don't they, um... allowances –
compassionate – for things like this?

BEX. Waste of time – always was. Can't fix stupid.

LORI. You're not.

BEX *shrugs*.

You're not stupid. Stop saying that.

BEX. No, I am. Nothing sticks. Can't focus. Can't remember
any of it.

LORI. So we made plans for that.

BEX. Fuck off.

LORI. Structure your time. Eat properly.

BEX. For one minute.

LORI. Exercise. Sleep. Build a routine.

BEX. Why though? No, I mean it – genuinely why? Cos it
never ends. GCSEs and NVQs and BTECs and HNDs. Do
this one, then that. No, you can't get that piece of paper until

you've got this one. No, we don't offer that here. No, not around shift work. You don't meet our basic criteria. How long have you been out of education? Saddle yourself with what – fifteen grand of debt – twenty, thirty, by the time you've done all of it – all to go chasing after jobs that don't even exist? What's the point?

LORI. To do something better.

BEX. What's better?

LORI. We're doing it. We're so close.

BEX. Y'know I was actually happy before – before you came and told me how shitty my life was.

LORI. You were miserable.

BEX. No, you told me I was miserable. You told me so often I started to believe it.

LORI. No –

BEX. You *made* me miserable. You make my life unbearable just by the way you look at it. You know all you had to do today was breeze in and say 'well done' – take a look around and be even the tiniest bit impressed, not immediately start trying to fix things – but it's *impossible* – physically impossible for you – because nothing about my life is ever good enough.

LORI. I've only been trying to help.

BEX. Fuck your help. None of this is by accident. Smiley potato faces because we had them for Christmas dinner one year after Mum incinerated the roasties and we never looked back. Onion rings because the engagement ring Dad got didn't fit her right at first, so he ran out for a bag of these instead. Burnt half the skin off her finger but she couldn't stop laughing. We've got Sunny Delight that I had to order from fucking eBay because that's the right one. Everything here is for her. I didn't think I had stories like yours but I do.

LORI (*weakly*). I just thought you might want a range.

BEX. She'd never touch it.

LORI. I know.

BEX. So why would you...? It's about paying respects. This is fucking communion shit. You don't mess with that.

LORI. I understand.

BEX. You don't. It's my fault. This is my fault. Should've been up front with you. Shouldn't have let it get this far. But you don't get to sit with us. You don't belong at this table and you never will. That's okay. But it's enough now.

Into –

15. THEN

LORI *is drunk.*

LORI. Bex! Bex! Where are you?

BEX. Hey.

LORI. Hey – you're still up.

BEX. Yeah.

LORI. Great.

BEX. You weren't answering my calls.

LORI. Sorry.

BEX. Where have you been?

LORI. Sorry.

BEX. Do you know what time it is?

LORI. Shall we have a drink?

BEX. No thanks.

LORI. Little drink?

BEX. I'm not –

LORI. Cheeky little nightcap.

BEX. I'll get you some water.

LORI. Fuck off.

BEX. Can I talk to you?

LORI. Me first. We're celebrating.

BEX. No.

LORI. Yes. Have we got fizz? Nothing cold, right? Okay, so
     that's another rule – a new rule, add it to your list – fizz in
     the fridge at all times, in case of emergencies.

BEX. Do you want to sit down?

LORI. Right. Gotta be whiskey then.

BEX. Please.

LORI. Okay – it's late – I'm sorry – I'm terrible. I've got to talk
     to you.

BEX. I need to –

LORI. I've found it. The most fucking perfect... You know the
     dodgy chicken shop on South Street? Finally being put out of
     its misery. And so I know what you're thinking – too small –
     much too small – and yes, you are correct – but the bookie
     next door that's been closed for a million years? Same
     landlord. We can knock through, tart it up, make it
     incredible.

BEX. Uh-huh.

LORI. Perfect. I promise you it's perfect.

BEX (*quietly*). Great.

LORI. So, will you wipe that look off your face and have a
     drink with me now?

BEX. I've got something I need to tell you too.

LORI. I know. You said, and I've got... (*Glancing at her phone.*) Seventeen missed calls? Wow. Needy much?

BEX. You weren't answering, so...

LORI. I'm sorry. I'll make it up to you. Come on – a toast to us, and to the future, and then we'll get on to your thing. (*Beat.*) What? Jesus Christ, Bex, who died?

A horrible silence. Into –

16. NOW

LORI. Okay. Right, I'll... I'm just going to go then.

BEX. Yeah.

LORI. And you can do what you want with... Chuck all the... Or don't, actually – give it to some homeless –

BEX. No homeless person wants a pulled-jackfruit wrap.

LORI. Uh-huh. And you'd know, would you?

BEX. Fiver says so.

LORI. Right. Because of course you're an expert on every sort of... Forget it.

BEX. Thanks for trying though.

LORI. Actually I can't... You're grieving, so you get a free pass on a lot of this, but that is a... a very classist attitude. A very... People can surprise you. Give them a chance and people will surprise you.

BEX. Okay.

LORI. Not everybody wants the shit they're given – most people – the vast majority of people – they're not actively choosing the shit they're given, they're just given it – no other option.

I tried to give you another option, and that makes me the villain, apparently. For offering something better.

BEX. Who says your stuff is better?

LORI. I'm done with this. I can't argue with you.

BEX. Go on. Who?

LORI. It is. It just is, Bex. Objectively. Um. Ethically – nutritionally – sustainably. Better for you, better for the planet, better for the people who make it – not that you've ever seemed to give a fuck about them. Do you want carbon footprint, or fairly traded, pesticide-free, low-impact, vitamin-rich... what sort of metric are you after? It's better.

BEX. If you say so.

LORI. Stop trying to make it some heritage thing, some cultural thing – diabetes isn't a protected characteristic. I am so tired of this.

BEX. Of trying to make me better?

LORI. Yes.

Pause.

BEX. Lot of judgement coming from a pisshead.

LORI. I'm not... I told you, I'm managing that.

BEX. Your liver's gotta be way more fucked than my arteries, but that's fine. At least you don't drink the cheap stuff.

LORI. I'm dealing with it. I've said sorry for –

BEX. Good luck, anyway.

LORI. Okay. I hope tonight is... I will try to leave you alone but please know you can call me whenever you want to.

BEX. Can I ask you something?

LORI. Sure.

BEX. Did you ever want me like this, or did you only want the thing you thought you could make me into?

LORI. Of course I did. I just wanted you to have more.

BEX. More like you?

LORI. Just *more*! Happier, healthier, *more*! Isn't that the whole
point of…? And this – all this – I'm sorry, but I find it
grotesque. It's not a tribute. It's obscene, actually. Celebrate
the woman, not her cause of death. Do better. Every parent
wants their child to do better.

BEX. You didn't know her.

LORI. I'm not asking you to rewrite your personality. I'm not
asking you to turn your back on the people who raised you.
I'm just asking you to do… something. If it's not the
restaurant, fine. If it's not with me, so be it, okay, because I
can't keep doing this. Plant a forest. Write a novel –

BEX. What?

LORI. Or whatever.

BEX. When have you seen me read a novel?

LORI. But suggesting that you do something – *anything* – that
you don't drop out of college for a second time, that you take
yourself seriously and figure out what it is you love – that
doesn't make me a bad person, it doesn't make me a snob, and
it doesn't make you a class traitor. It makes me a really good
girlfriend, actually. So tell me what I've done wrong. Tell me
why trying to be better is a bad thing. (*Beat.*) Bex? I'm waiting.

Silence.

BEX. It's not… I'm sorry. I know it's not useful to be sorry, but
I am. I'm sorry I can't make you understand it. It's hard to
pinpoint exactly what it is – because you've got this way,
this really clever way of making everything sound so
reasonable when you say it and then I think I've got
everything straight when you're not here – I've got a handle
on it all – but I can't…

The thing is you can't tell me I have this capacity to be better
without telling me I'm shit right now – making me feel like
shit. Without going 'Jesus Christ, look at the state of you, but

take my hand and pull your socks up and we'll get through
it.' And you do it in this really patient, caring, compassionate
way – like you do really feel for me, and how shit my life is,
and you want to swoop in and whisk me off to this brave
new world of matcha powder and pomegranates and
reclaimed floorboards, and… And that isn't…

What if I really was happy as I am? Nothing would terrify
you more. Happy before you got to work on me, making me
fit for your oyster bars and supper clubs and Christmases
with your family. Happy without changing a hair – can you
imagine the power of that? Can you imagine how incredible
it'd be if that were true? And I'm not. Of course I'm not!
What do you expect? And I'm not saying things aren't shit –
my life isn't shit – but it doesn't mean… Aaargh! I can see
the argument – it's there – it's flickering, but I can't quite…
I'm hungry. I've not eaten. Sorry.

Did you ever stop to think about why my life is shit before
you started trying to fix things? My life is shit because the
system is shit. Because the job market is shit. Because
housing is shit. Because no one on minimum wage and zero
hours has the headspace to make their own yogurt. And the
only solution you can offer is for me to drag myself out of it –
to upgrade – to somehow become a less shit person and then
the world will open up before me. So I can get off the estate,
clean up my act, fix my hair, and then once you've ironed all
the kinks out of me, if I ever have to talk about where I'm
from, or where I'm *from*-from, it can be with this big fat line
drawn underneath it, like thank fuck you got to me when you
did. Thank fuck you saved me. Thank fuck I'm better now.

I think it's a waste of time trying to make people better. I
know that sounds bad, but I do. I think people are always
going to be people – kind and stupid and greedy and
everything else between. But what you can change is the
things around them. Not just saying 'be a better person – be
the type of person who deserves better', but saying actually if
this is… If this is… Cos if I move off the estate, someone else
moves in. I get promoted, someone else takes my old spot. So

you've gotta improve the estate, right, not the individual? But you can't see that. You aren't interested in that version of better. And I think maybe the proper goal of all this self-improvement – all social climbing, in your eyes – is just to get to the point where you personally don't know any poor people any more. They're still there – you sort of abstractly know that – but they don't keep you awake at night. Cos it's not you – you're not them – and everyone you know is fine.

Who is it really for? What difference would it have made? Would she still be alive – my mum – if she were more like you? Richer, quieter, whiter? Doctors would've been kinder to her, listened better, taken her more seriously. She could've hired a dietician – a personal trainer – a lifestyle coach. She would've had different tastes – learnt to eat better growing up. Or maybe not. Plenty of fat posh people. But she'd have carried it differently – dressed better – wouldn't get the same kind of stares. People might've still thought she was thick but they might've hated her less for it. Maybe she'd have made it. Had an epiphany. Turned it all around. But maybe you can't make people better. What's better, anyway?

Y'know she was always big – always had an appetite – but it only really became a problem when she felt like she had to hide it. That's when it got bad. That's what you did to her – people like you – you made her feel ashamed. And when you feel shame you seek comfort, and when you feel lesser you seek comfort, and when you feel judged for every choice you ever made and every choice that was already made for you… (*Gestures to the food around them.*) This isn't what killed her, this is what made her life worth living. You're what killed her. You. And you made me feel ashamed too – not just of myself, ashamed of her. Ashamed of this incredible woman – this kind, generous, loving… Who always had a seat at her table. Who would try anything once. Who lived more than you ever will even if you reach a hundred. She didn't want to change. She shouldn't have to. She would've been happy if only people had just *left her alone*.

And yeah, I know, it's all a con – she didn't really want it, she just got tricked into wanting it. It's this whole institutionalised, weaponised class warfare that teaches us to know our place, and take what we're given, and says 'Oh no, you don't want this – you'll never get them to eat that.' So we go 'Yeah, fuck your fancy shit – it's not for us – give us our nuggets.' We eat shit because we're treated like shit and we're all too thick to know any better, but you – you're not like that. No, you're different. You're one of the good guys. You wanted me to try everything – even the rank stuff – you said I deserved the best. Did you really believe it? But it doesn't matter, because if the best's not on offer it makes no difference whether I'm deserving. It's actually worse. It's cruel to make me want it. I'm me and you're you, so… so that's all there is to it. Waste of time. I'm right. I know I'm right. Tell me I'm right.

You can't make people better, but what if I was enough already? What if we just had to find the compromise? Is it this? Is it exactly this, me and you and a weird little well-intentioned, culturally insensitive neighbourhood restaurant? All micro herbs and community gardens and pride flags and Stormzy on the playlist? We'll do it up in matching dungarees, and it'll be slow to start cos people don't know us, but we build trust, we get the word out. You bring in the yoga mums and I go round the barbershops and nail salons with boxes of wings to drum up custom. It's a weird mix, but it works. We're a family. Queer kids come in to do their homework and paint their nails in secret. Homeless know they'll get fed, no questions asked. And if you're ever locking up late by yourself there's always someone insists on walking you home – 'Don't worry auntie, we've gotta get you back to your girl.' Like it's no big thing. No one bothers us. And we get awards and plaudits and all that but we don't care, and when some slick dickhead comes round with a shiny suit and an expansion plan you kick him out. I say 'You didn't have to do that' and you say 'Who needs it? This is us.' And you kiss me and the world explodes. No one else thought we could do it, but you did, and we do. We do. We do.

Do you like the sound of it? You should – it was all your idea – your little wet dream of gentrification. I've gone over it so many times I think it's pretty perfect now. Only there's no money, and no community, and the yoga mums are racist and the barbershops are homophobic and my mum is dead so what's the point of anything? You can't make it better. You can't make any of this better. And I try not to think about it any more because it just makes me so sad.

I don't know what I want. That was always the worst thing. It would be so much easier to walk away if I had something to walk towards, and I don't. I don't want to write a novel. I don't want to run a restaurant, not really. Never did. I don't have a... a passion for animals, or a longing for the great outdoors, or any sort of... and that made me think I was stupid and broken and it's the kind of thing you can't admit to anyone so it was easier to just let you make plans for both of us, but it's gone too far now. You want to make me better – you do – but it's only ever been on your terms. You want me to blossom into something else and I think that's love – I genuinely think it is – but it's not reasonable. Love is unreasonable, maybe, but I just want to feel like enough, and I don't – not when I'm with you. I feel like I'm failing, and that was you. It's not me, it's you. And if I can't find a way to love you and love myself at the same time then I know what I have to do, because this can't be what it should feel like. Like I'm always having to hold my breath when I'm around you.

I'm sorry. I'm sorry I didn't tell you any of this sooner. I'm sorry I can't even tell you all this now. It's too exhausting. It'd take too long. You wouldn't understand. That's okay, but that's on you. Let that be your burden. I'll be fine. I'm young. I'm smart. I'm hot. I was always enough – that was your mistake. Maybe my mistake as well. It's okay to want different things, value different things, but I value myself, so... You can't fix something that isn't broken. I refuse to break.

LORI. Bex? Are you okay? You haven't said anything for a really long time.

BEX. Yeah, I'm fine. Just hungry. I'll be fine.

Into –

17. THEN

LORI *starts making* BEX *her impressive snack. It's possibly the first real food we've seen. It's maybe something like a grilled cheese sandwich. It should look and smell delicious.* LORI *also has a drink for herself.*

BEX. You really don't have to go to all this trouble.

LORI. No trouble.

BEX. Honestly. I would've been happy with the Pot Noodle.

LORI. Then you need to love yourself more.

BEX. Don't worry, I love myself plenty.

LORI. Just don't expect this every time we work together.

BEX. You'd have me back then? (*Beat.*) Am I getting an egg?

LORI. Everything's better with an egg.

BEX. What else have you got?

LORI. Taleggio. Some Comté. Lincolnshire Poacher for bite.

BEX. Fancy.

LORI. Haven't even got to the truffle honey.

BEX. My mum used to do me toasties when I was sick – still does sometimes. Ham and cheese and Heinz tomato soup. Gotta be Heinz.

LORI. Great taste.

BEX. Yeah, she's alright.

LORI. Shouldn't really be eating this late – certainly not this – but… I don't know. I think everything tastes better after midnight.

BEX. So true.

LORI. Yeah?

BEX. Chicken nuggets on the night bus – can't beat it.

LORI. If you knew where those chickens had… (*Stops herself.*) Sorry, that's not…

BEX. That bit going spare?

LORI. Keep your fingers out!

BEX. Just helping you tidy up.

LORI. Stop it!

BEX. Hot chocolate – that's another one. Hot chocolate, penguin biscuit – you nibble the ends off two corners –

LORI. Suck through it like a straw!

BEX. Yes!

LORI. Even better with a Club.

BEX. Noted.

LORI. Midnight feasts – can't beat them. Magic. Terrible for your digestion but great for the soul. That's the thing – it's more than fuel, it's comfort, it's care, it's… a salve against the injustices of the world. (*Beat.*) Sorry – I'm being a massive wanker, apparently. I'm not always like this.

BEX. No?

LORI. Maybe I am. I don't know – shit at first impressions. Anyway, right. Here we go. It'll be pretty hot in the middle, so… Go ahead. I won't watch you eat – that'd be weird. I'm going to go and check in on… Hope you like it. Let me know if… Bon appétit. Fuck's sake. Sorry. Enjoy.

BEX. Thank you.

LORI *smiles awkwardly and goes.* BEX *grins. She looks at the sandwich. She takes a big bite. Maybe we watch her eat the whole thing. It's good. She is happy.*

End.

Notes on the Food
Chris Bush

These aren't recipes as such, but I've thought a lot about the food in this show (I think a lot about food in general), so here are a few notes and things you might want to try.

Chocolate marquise with a basil fluid gel

A chocolate marquise is a very fancy, very rich French dessert somewhere between a mousse and a ganache. You set it in a terrine and cut off slabs of it. It's one of those recipes that gets described as 'challenging' and makes the judges on *MasterChef* frown apprehensively. It's far too complicated for you to want a recipe from me. Similarly, fluid gels require weird science-y ingredients like agar agar or xanthan gum, and I absolutely do not have time for that.

However, chocolate and basil *works*. So, make a chocolate dessert of your choice – a good brownie perhaps, a fondant, a flourless torte, or just rich chocolate pots made with equal quantities of melted dark chocolate and double cream, flavoured with a pinch of salt, a dash of vanilla and a splash of booze (I'd always go for amaretto). Serve with a scoop of mascarpone sweetened slightly with icing sugar and run through with flecks of freshly chopped basil, and some roasted strawberries. Roasted strawberries are great. Just halve your fruits, toss with a little salt, fresh black pepper, demerara sugar, olive oil and balsamic vinegar, and roast in a medium-high oven for 15–20 minutes. Rich dark chocolate, jammy, peppery strawberries, and cooling aromatic mascarpone – this will make you look very fancy and taste excellent.

Turmeric chicken with Scotch bonnet aioli and kohlrabi slaw in an activated-charcoal flatbread

There's nothing here that shouldn't work. Always use chicken thighs instead of breast, ideally on the bone. Marinate your chicken pieces in yogurt and lemon juice (or just use buttermilk), along with crushed garlic, salt, pepper, cumin, paprika and a hefty dose of turmeric. Refrigerate overnight then bake in a hot oven and strip the meat from the bone.

Aioli (garlic mayonnaise) can be made easily with an immersion blender or food processor. Start with one egg and one egg yolk, salt, 4–5 crushed cloves of garlic and as much fresh Scotch bonnet as you fancy (start sparingly, you can always add more) in the base of a blender. Add a couple of tablespoons of olive oil and pulse to combine. Then slowly trickle in another 150–200ml of olive oil with the blender running until a thick, emulsified aioli forms.

Kohlrabi is technically a cabbage. Peel it, grate it, make slaw out of it alongside whatever other vegetables you like – perhaps carrot and red cabbage for colour, and some matchsticks of apple if you're feeling fancy. Some mint and coriander would be good here too. Don't dress it with mayonnaise if you've already got your aioli, maybe just some lime juice, sesame oil, salt and pepper.

Flatbreads are great and the easiest thing in the world to make. Get whatever flour you want – maybe 50/50 plain and wholemeal. Season with salt, pepper, and whatever flavourings you enjoy – I go for whole spices like cumin, nigella, mustard and fennel seeds, and a pinch of chilli flakes. You can add a teaspoon of your activated charcoal here if you're a dickhead. Add warm water at a ratio of roughly 2:1 flour to water and knead for around 5 minutes, or until you get bored, to form a not-sticky, pliable dough. Rest for 30 minutes, divide into walnut-sized balls, roll out each ball as thinly as you possibly can and toast in a dry, hot pan for 1–2 minutes each side until they have some good colour (another good reason not to add charcoal like a dickhead).

Assemble your shredded chicken, slaw and aioli inside your wrap and enjoy. Do I actually expect you to make this? No. Would it taste great if you did? Almost certainly yes.

Pickled turnips, sprout tops and cobnuts

This sounds a bit too virtuous to be enjoyable, but it could actually be quite nice. Pickled vegetables are a great thing to have sitting in your fridge. A quick pickling liquor uses a 2:2:1 ratio of water, vinegar (I use white wine vinegar) and sugar brought to a boil along with salt and whatever aromatics you like, such as peppercorns, coriander seeds, mustard seeds, bay leaves, etc. (I like sweet pickles, but you can reduce the sugar or cut it out entirely if you so desire.) Prep your vegetables – in this instance, peel and cube your turnips – place them in sterilised jars and pour the pickling liquid on top of them. You can also add a few pieces of beetroot to each jar to dye your turnips a shocking neon pink, but I think Lori would be too classy for this. Once cool, pop lids on the jars and keep them in the fridge until desired.

Actually, if I was going to convince you to make one thing, it would be homemade pink pickled onions. Finely slice a whole bunch of red onions and pop them in jars along with some sliced red chillies and whole peeled cloves of garlic. Cover with your pickling liquor. Put them on everything, but especially fried eggs and avocado. Thank me later. But I digress...

Toast your cobnuts (or hazelnuts) in a dry pan. Set aside, add a splash of rapeseed oil to your pan and briefly cook your shredded sprout tops (or spring greens/kale/cavolo nero – some form of leafy brassica). Dress the leaves in a simple mustard vinaigrette and top with your pickled turnips and toasted cobnuts. If you're not salivating at the thought of this, adorn with chunks of a good, squidgy blue cheese and suddenly this might become something you actually want to eat.

Charred sprouts with bacon and chimichurri

Yeah, these would bang, but you don't need a recipe for it. Never boil a sprout, it's a hate crime. Frying is okay but roasting is better. In fact, there's not a single vegetable that isn't improved by roasting it and this is the hill I will die on.

Fish stew, Normandy-style, green-bean salad, Rice Krispie brownies

You want a proper recipe for all of this, not my ramblings, but it'll be worth it. A Normandy fish stew will be full of mussels and white fish, with a sauce made from cider, fish stock and crème fraîche. Toasting breadcrumbs in garlic butter to put on top is obviously an inspired addition.

Green beans want boiling for less time than you think. I believe life is too short to faff around with plunging vegetables into ice water once you've cooked them, whatever real chefs might say. Instead, fry up some lardon/bacon bits in the same pan you toasted your garlicky breadcrumbs in, then finish off your drained green beans by sautéing them with the bacon. Does this really count as a salad? I simply do not care.

Nigella is the queen of brownies, just follow any of her recipes (although I often find they need slightly longer to cook than she says). Personally I favour her standard brownie recipe, with the addition of some dollops of peanut butter, broken Biscoff biscuits and a sprinkle of flaky salt added on top of the brownie batter just before baking if you're trying to show off.

Roasted plantain with chip-shop spice, Dublin Bay prawns with gumbo butter

Chip Spice is Hull's contribution to global gastronomy. This paprika-based seasoning would absolutely work with plantain, although clearly Lori would be better off frying them.

Gumbo butter is something of a contradiction. A lot of Cajun and Creole cuisine (such as gumbo) is built around a roux, but rather than the pale French emulsion of butter and flour, a Cajun roux cooks flour with scalding hot vegetable oil until it turns a deep chocolatey brown. Vegetable oil has a much higher smoke point than butter, meaning it can be brought to a much higher temperature and cooked for longer, creating a darker, more complex flavour. A real gumbo would never use butter, so Lori isn't being very authentic here, but then that's kind of the point.

So I imagine this dish would involve Dublin Bay prawns seared on a grill and dressed with a brown butter (butter cooked slowly until the milk solids caramelise and it turns a nutty, toasty brown) infused with cayenne pepper, smoked paprika, garlic and the Cajun 'Holy Trinity' of green pepper, celery and white onion. And yes, this sounds excellent.

Tea-smoked hogget

I have never made anything like this. I absolutely should not be trusted around fire pits. On paper I feel like it should work though. I can tell you that tea-smoking is a real and delicious thing, and works well with duck and chicken. You don't need a proper smoker to do this, but can use a wok double-lined with tin foil instead. It's worth trying, but you should definitely find a real recipe for it.

Lori's toastie

There are two versions of this toastie – the one we make in the show (which is delicious), and the properly extravagant one there wasn't enough time to cook in the scene.

Version one is a sort of eggy bread/toastie hybrid. Dip two slices of bread in beaten egg (seasoned with salt, pepper, optional finely grated garlic and parmesan) and fry them in a pan with foaming butter until the bottom sides have some colour. Then flip one slice, top with the grated cheese of your choice (and a drizzle of truffle honey if you have it to hand), and add your second slice of bread on top, the uncooked side facing up. Leave for a minute, then flip the whole sandwich so all sides of the bread have had direct contact with the pan. Add extra butter to the pan as needed, and remember to press down your toastie with a spatula or fish slice to achieve good colour.

The second, more elaborate toastie requires three slices of bread – two thin and one thick. Use a cookie cutter to cut a disc out of the centre of your thick slice of bread. Butter all three slices on both sides. Place your holey slice and one normal slice into your frying pan, adding an extra knob of butter in the hole. Carefully crack an egg into the hole, and partially cover the pan with a lid, encouraging the white of the egg to set from above as well as cook from below. As soon as your egg is cooked enough to flip over, first flip your regular slice of bread and top with half your cheese. Then very carefully flip your eggy slice trying very hard not to break the yolk, and place on top of your cheesy slice, and once this is done add your third slice to the pan. As soon as this has some colour, add your remaining cheese on top of the eggy slice, and your third slice of bread on top of that, uncooked side facing up. Now flip the whole thing and cook the final side. What you should now have is a triple-layer sandwich which goes bread > cheese > bread-with-runny-egg-centre > more cheese > bread. This is going to take a few attempts to get right but it will be one of the best things you've ever eaten. Oh, and you can put pink pickled onions on it as well. Sorted.

A Nick Hern Book

Hungry first published in Great Britain in 2021 as a paperback original by Nick Hern Books Limited, The Glasshouse, 49a Goldhawk Road, London W12 8QP, in association with Paines Plough and Belgrade Theatre Coventry

Hungry copyright © 2021 Chris Bush

Cover photograph: Rebecca Nead-Menear; graphic design: Michael Windsor-Ungureanu

Designed and typeset by Nick Hern Books, London
Printed in the UK by Mimeo Ltd, Huntingdon, Cambridgeshire PE29 6XX

A CIP catalogue record for this book is available from the British Library

ISBN 978 1 83904 011 5

www.nickhernbooks.co.uk

facebook.com/nickhernbooks

twitter.com/nickhernbooks